Parkinson's Journey

Karen Fillmore Nave

Poems about having the disease
and how to deal with it

Copyright 2013
Karen Fillmore Nave
All rights reserved
ISBN-13:978-1482546002
ISBN-10:1482546000

Thanks to author LeAnne Hardy for her editing expertise. Thanks to my friend and colleague Michelle Rowe Johnson for helping me through the differences between aging and Parkinson's. Thank you to my husband Dan for helping to edit, keeping up with the minerals, vitamins, and ideas to ease my symptoms, and standing by me on this long journey.

June

One day almost gone
Sense of smell, voice range, laughter
Disappearing points

Charley horse in bed
As I turned over sleeping
Awakening pain

Trembling fingers drum
Dancing to their own rhythm
Cradled in my hand

Wall braced hand shook me
Disturbing conversation
Leaving PD clues

Parkinson's disease
With a tale-telling tremor
Is now my story

The cramping surprise
Curling inward posture, fight!
Stretch to your limits!

My whispers feel loud
But you can't hear me until
We sing my voice back

The organizer-
Instigator, may change roles
With my care partner

Adult children fear
Loss of their childhood image
Resisting my world

My face, a sad blank
Does not always reflect the
Happiness within

Tightness of throat base
And breath squashed out of chest walls
Scares me to a stop

Left, left, marching arm
Keeping rhythm with right leg
Slowly rewiring

Loud confrontations
Shimmy and shake my body
Feeling overload

Pain is the signal
To relax, stretch, breathe deeply
And release the mind

Parkinson's disease
By necessity is an
Assemblage point shift

Lead legs drag up stairs
Breathing deeply from the gut
Free thoughts free the legs

Gene pool potpourri
Life training anxiety
Disrupt neurology

July

Chest tightening squeeze
Panic fires through my brain
As I climbed the stairs

Chattering brain loops
Freeze future development
Stuck in perceptions

Life with less tension,
Less indignation, less fear,
Citalopram calm

Spasmodic gestures
Frighten and open me to
Ridicule, pity

Doubt glues me in place
There are too many choices
Routines free spirit

Reevaluate
Is it worth the consequences
Of just being right?

The couch is safe-base
Where I can rejuvenate
From intense cramping

Interpretations
Of my brain are painfully
Misplaced connections

Do lonely people
Hoard their deep distress in piles
Of indecisions?

Do not scare yourself
Practice your best smile daily
Eyes shining brightly

Calming the fear, and
Understanding one's true self
Is the PD goal

August

I've had too much stress
When fingers stiffen and ache
And Dan leads me home

Hunting for the key
To changing and containing
Parkinson's weird truths

Temperatures stress
As do angry attitudes
And cold denials

How far can I change
How I view the world and me?
Will I change PD?

The tremor doesn't
Bother me; I can adapt
To zigzag patterns

The left keyboard strokes
Are missing in my hand thoughts
Give up or practice

Tension distractions
Ease the way, smiles, gentle talk
Life observations

When the inner voice
Is a chattering puppet
Tell it to sit down

We are all fighting
Great battles to win our peace
And find our normal

Living a bubble
Where drama does not touch me
To push my limits

Ain't it awful! With
Friends like you to depress m
Who needs enemies?

September

I reach out to others
Expanding my safety zone
And wanting balance

A burst of anger
Or of fear, jars the system
Into reactions

The love language of
Presence, smiling eyes, warm touch
Knit my wellbeing

Laughter Yoga gives
Dopamine to caregivers
Bless them, they need it

Depression squeezes
Daily household decisions
Partners need care too

So angry I'm rude
About a poor mammogram
Threatening cancer

Picking up marbles
With toes that refuse to grip
Challenging balance

Yoga pushes me
Farther than I'd do alone
Breathing and stretching

Your emergencies
Are no longer mine to solve
I respond slowly

Stored anxiety
Catches me on commercials
Racing my tremor

Eyes slow to focus
I'm searching for range in print
Scanning mysteries

October

I move through doorways
Then forget what I'm after
And start fresh again

Avoiding drama
Has made me more resilient
To emotion swings

Guarded energy
Is doled out in timed minutes
Of accomplishments

All PD symptoms
Appear and leave by degree
Intense to normal

I feel quite myself
At times throughout the day 'til
Parts of me time out

Practicing daily
Realigning, chin back, to
Swallow pills later

Hunting for words to
Explain, and finding spaces
In my thought process

Joy and gratitude
Change expressions immensely
On friends with PD

Feeling small, hiding,
Silent, letting conflicts pass
Like a sudden squall

Arthritis stabs hands
Without locking position
Unlike PD toes

Two cup day morning!
Sun bright on stadium walls
And on passing smiles

Stopped wearing heavy
Wrist jarring watch, easier
Time by cell phone light

Thumb weakening change
Pressure missing for clippers
Adaptions to life

Saying "Good Morning!"
Inspires people cheerfully
And 'wakens my face

Eyes tire easily
Print piles up in stacks unread
Sight dictates pass-times

Unexpected age
Speeding through my body-mind
Please give wisdom too!

Relaxing my toes
Might mean flexing them hard tight
Against the cramping

November

Grateful you hear me
Over my frenetic hand
Seeking attention

Observing myself
Talking to you, is as strange
To me, as to you

I'm feeling nauseous
From tightly strung neck muscles
Extremities quake

I am distracted
Easily or absorbed to
Painful condition

Skipping exercise
Is not an option if I
Want computer time

Left pulsing tremor
Plays with balance and stillness
In yoga postures

Learning to release
My choices, before they chew
On my back muscles

I jerk and start when
Extending my arm from bed
In defiant thrust

Panting at my desk
After opening building,
Forty one doors, breathe

Feel grabbed by the scruff
Then shook by the PD dog
And dropped on my couch

I am still awake
With a dull aching arm that
Won't rest and grows weak

Dropping things of late
Treasured gift of myrtle bowl
Patched with jagged scar

Finding patience and
An expectancy to days
In this calmer life

A cacophony
Of words do not make them true
Or easy to hear

Peeling toes and ears
Shedding skin daily like burns
Odd realities

Leave it on the floor
All body expectations
Of proficiency

Visualizing
Round clocks to focus my sight
For my brain to see

Condescension riles
Don't assume our limits and
Treat us like infants

Uneasy feeling
Of things not right, unsureness
In abilities

Reprogramming me
With minerals, movement and
Meaningful purpose

Drama over fires
Our bodies with impulses
We cannot control

Erupting tremors
After accusative blasts
Imagining calm

Stuffing emotions
I used to know my anger
When my toes were cold

December

Is apprehension
A drama curse? Can it flip
To expectations?

Kneeling is easy
Rising gracefully off the
Floor is challenging

Drama vampires
Suck the life from their partners
How can they not know?

Some things you just do
Without reservation fear
Because it is you

Describing drama
Is a pointless example
To a dramatic

A friend plays tennis
But standing in line waiting
She loses balance

Right foot feels the floor
Left foot is on razor edge
Yoga balancing

Poems appear at two
Swirling night thoughts of the day
Captured, then I sleep

Life crossroads narrow
How do I find my pathway
Without outside work?

Sun rays through skylight
Playing with me and catching
Shining my corners

Why is waiting hard?
Anticipating movement
Tremor cramping limbs

January

New resolution
Of my daily gratitudes
Inspire happiness

Mending heels on socks
Equal work accomplishments
Reasons to be proud

Comfort, gratitude
In everyday things, places
Change is coming soon

Journal of blessings
Grounds me in the present time
Letting go of if...

Like starry rivers
Floors shining, reflecting lights
Times of the past life

Watching strength of legs
Remembering old power
Now as fortitude

Fear of change, I pray
This God or something better
Give me a purpose

Surprise, life's not done!
PD personality
A revelation

Judged far too harshly
Painting, writing, needle work
Let the gift flow free

Stage two Parkinson's
Is overwhelmed by symptoms
Levodopa time

Desperate and glad
They go to brain surgery
To lose their symptoms

Back to try again
Weight Watchers, Nordic Walking
Old friends left in fear

Two AM awake
Is not the same as morning's
Probabilities

Having to recheck
Incomplete surprises left
On countertops, desks…

Curious digit
Left thumb stands to attention
When I talk and walk

The freezing gets her
As she tries to walk doorways
Feet tapping in place

Intermittent lapse
Fingers, arm, leg, toes, bladder
Lack of strength wears one

February

Left hand reaching back
Eyes seeking blind spot in view
Relearning habits

Intense PD look
I am not angry at you
My face scares me too

Leg bouncing rhythm
Of a woodpecker tapping
Urgency response

One cannot be scared
Fear cascades muscle cramping
Be calm, carry on

Smiling eyes hold me
Safely moored to the brown couch
In the PD sea

Made in the USA
Lexington, KY
11 September 2017